Buildings

Jordan McGill

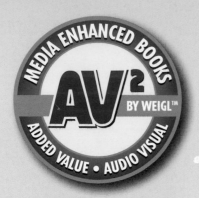

Go to **www.av2books.com**, and enter this book's unique code.

BOOK CODE

L680284

AV² by Weigl brings you media enhanced books that support active learning.

AV² provides enriched content that supplements and complements this book. Weigl's AV² books strive to create inspired learning and engage young minds in a total learning experience.

Your AV² Media Enhanced books come alive with...

Audio
Listen to sections of the book read aloud.

Video
Watch informative video clips.

Embedded Weblinks
Gain additional information for research.

Try This!
Complete activities and hands-on experiments.

Key Words
Study vocabulary, and complete a matching word activity.

Quizzes
Test your knowledge.

Slide Show
View images and captions, and prepare a presentation.

... and much, much more!

Published by AV² by Weigl
350 5th Avenue, 59th Floor New York, NY 10118
Website: www.av2books.com   www.weigl.com

Library of Congress Cataloging-in-Publicataion Data available upon request.
Fax 1-866-44-WEIGL for the attention of the Publishing Records department.

ISBN 978-1-61690-949-9 (hard cover)
ISBN 978-1-61913-007-4 (soft cover)

Printed in the United States of America in North Mankato, Minnesota
2 3 4 5 6 7 8 9 0 16 15 14 13 12

112012
WEP311012

Project Coordinator: Jordan McGill Art Director: Terry Paulhus

Weigl acknowledges Getty Images as the primary image supplier for this title.

2

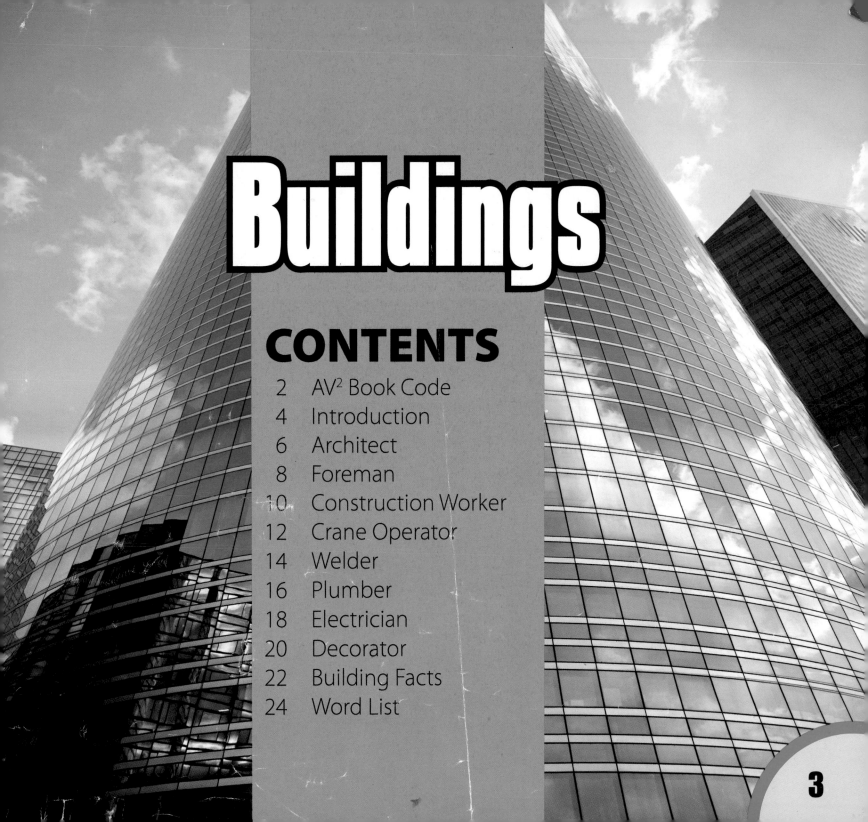

Buildings

CONTENTS

Some workers in our community put buildings together.

Architect

Electrician

Plumber

Welder

Foreman

Decorator

Construction Worker

Crane Operator

I plan how buildings will look.

6

I am an architect.

I make sure people are safe while they work.

I am a foreman.

I build buildings.

I am a construction worker.

I lift heavy objects high up.

I am a crane operator.

I make sure pieces
of metal stay in place.

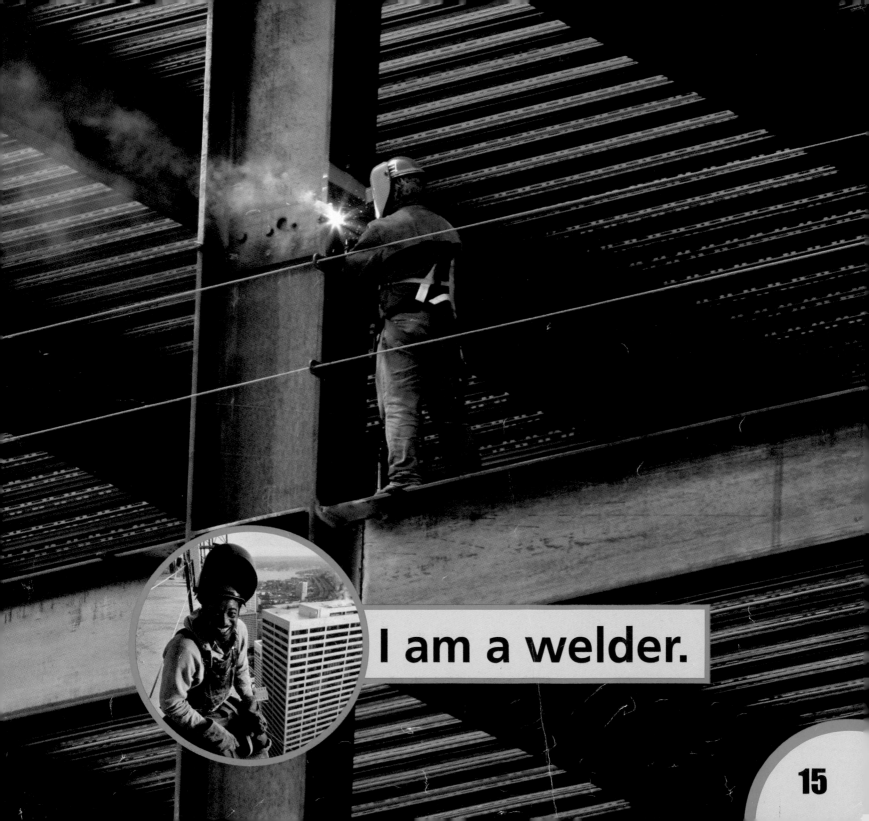

I am a welder.

I help water get to different parts of the building.

I am a plumber.

I wire the building for power and keep the lights on.

I am an electrician.

I decorate the inside of the building.

I am a decorator.

BUILDING FACTS

People with common interests can form a community. Buildings are an important part of a community. Many people plays roles in the construction of a building.

Communities revolve around buildings. Buildings are where people live, work, eat, and obtain essential services. Communities of all kinds, whether small towns or large cities, are made of buildings. Many workers play an important part in constructing buildings.

Architects plan what a building will look like before construction begins. Architecture is a mixture of art and science. Buildings are designed to be stunning and visually interesting, but they must also be sturdy and stay standing. Architects must balance art and science to create beautiful structures.

Foremen ensure that all safety standards are met. They also make sure that construction of the building is on schedule and will be finished on time. Problems can occur on building sites. It is the foreman's job to think of ways to correct the problems.

Construction workers do most of the heavy lifting and assembly on a building site. Construction workers need to know how to use different tools, such as jackhammers, power drills, and nail guns. They use these tools to put the building together.

Cranes move heavy materials and machinery around the construction site. Crane operators are responsible for controlling cranes of all sizes that help put buildings together. Modern skyscrapers are many stories tall. Some rise more than 100 floors above the street. Without cranes to lift the heavy equipment to the upper floors, buildings would be much smaller than they are now.

Welders connect pieces of metal by applying heat to permanently join them. On construction sites, welders join metal beams and scaffolding that form the frame of the building. They do this at great heights, often more than 100 feet (30 meters) above the ground.

Plumbers install and repair water systems, heaters, and large appliances. They play an important role before and after the building is complete. Problems with water and heating systems, such as water leaks, can occur long after a building is complete, and it is a plumber's job to fix them.

Electricians bring electricity to buildings. They connect wires, fuses, outlets, circuit breakers, and many other parts to a city's power grid so that the building will have lights and electricity. Much like plumbers, electricians play an important role keeping a building running properly long after it is built.

Decorators design the interior of the building. They decide how each room of the building looks. They do this by picking out paint colors, furniture, and decorations for the rooms. An decorator makes the inside of a building look nice.

WORD LIST

Research has shown that as much as 65 percent of all written material published in English is made up of 300 words. These 300 words cannot be taught using pictures or learned by sounding them out. They must be recognized by sight. This book contains 33 common sight words to help young readers improve their reading fluency and comprehension. This book also teaches young readers several important content words, such as proper nouns. These words are paired with pictures to aid in learning and improve understanding.

Page	Sight Words First Appearance
4	in, our, put, some, together
6	how, I, look, will
7	an
8	are, make, people, they, while, work
9	a
12	high, up
14	of, place
16	different, get, help, parts, the, to, water
18	and, for, keep, lights, on

Page	Content Words First Appearance
4	buildings, community, workers
5	architect, construction, crane, decorator, electrician, foreman, operator, plumber, welder
12	objects
14	metal, pieces
18	lights, power

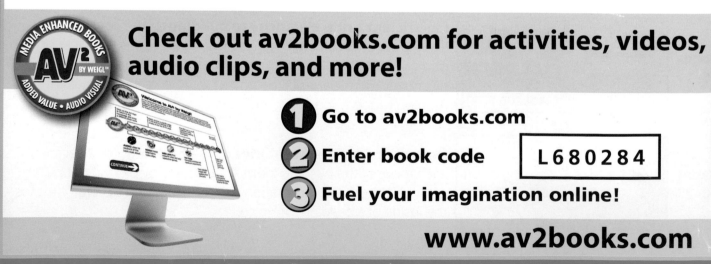

MEDIA ENHANCED BOOKS
AV2 BY WEIGL™
ADDED VALUE · AUDIO VISUAL

Check out av2books.com for activities, videos, audio clips, and more!

1 Go to av2books.com

2 Enter book code   L 6 8 0 2 8 4

3 Fuel your imagination online!

www.av2books.com